The Art of SKIING

1856-1936

Georges Lepape. *Woman's Home Companion.* 1928

The Art of SKIING

1856 -1936

TIMELESS, ENCHANTING ILLUSTRATIONS AND NARRATIVE
OF SKIING'S FORMATIVE YEARS

MAGAZINE COVERS AND ILLUSTRATIONS
PICTURE POSTCARDS
ADVERTISING ILLUSTRATIONS

GARY H. SCHWARTZ

❄

WOOD RIVER PUBLISHING
TIBURON,CALIFORNIA

The Art of Skiing
1856-1936

Wood River Publishing
680 Hawthorne Drive
Tiburon, California 94920

First Edition November 1989

Design: Gabrielle Disario
Editing: Susan Greer
Printing: Toppan Printing Co. Singapore

Library of Congress Cataloging in Publication Data:
89-50585
ISBN: 0-9623000-1-2

TABLE OF CONTENTS

INTRODUCTION 7

HISTORY OF SKIING 9

MAGAZINE ILLUSTRATIONS AND COVERS 19

    History of the Illustrated Magazine 21

    The Illustrations 24

ADVERTISING 69

    History of Advertising 71

    The Advertisements 74

POSTCARDS 101

    History of the Picture Postcard 102

    The Postcards 104

ACKNOWLEDGEMENTS 169

INDEX 171

Cover illustration: *The American Legion Monthly.*
Tenggren. 1933.

INTRODUCTION

"One peculiarity about ski running is that its followers never lose their enthusiasm. And small wonder — for it is indeed a glorious sport. There is everything in its favor. It takes one into the open air amid the finest scenery, it tests every faculty, it provides exercise for every muscle, and it gives health, strength, and pleasure beyond compare."

Munsey's Magazine
February, 1900

Artists, illustrators and photographers of the past have left behind a wonderfully visual world of graphic material depicting the evolution of skiing. What better way to appreciate how skiing has evolved to its eminent position in worldwide winter sports than by looking at the vehicles that originally brought the sport to the public: the magazine, the picture postcard, and advertising.

This volume begins in the mid-nineteenth century, during the infancy of both skiing and graphic illustration in the United States. It is a visual record of human ideas and social movements, as well as significant historical moments in the evolution of skiing. These works portray social, cultural and commercial fads and trends from the times of skiing pioneer "Snowshoe" Thompson in 1856 to the opening of America's first world-class ski resort, Sun Valley, Idaho, in 1936. You may be surprised to learn that magazine covers, postcards and even advertisements were designed with such imagination and beauty.

In the 1800s both skiing and graphic illustration were highly specialized but not yet available to the masses. As the cost of reproducing illustrations decreased, more magazine, postcard and advertising art related to skiing were offered to the growing middle class; hence the growth of the sport paralleled its increased popularity in the visual media.

New worlds were opened to people who "discovered" skiing through printed images. Each visual resource played an important part in the public's perception of skiing and definitely piqued the interests of many. The sport grew from one involving fewer than 30,000 American ski jumpers and outdoor enthusiasts in the 1920s to many millions today.

The works in this compilation show the cultural, social and commercial roles of the sport from 1856 to 1936, including changes in ski clothing, equipment, technique, resort development, and public perceptions. Some of the pictures depict skiing in a sensitive light at a time when it was largely an elite, amateur pastime in America. The public tended to associate skiing with romance and fashion. Many of the graphics have touches of sensuality, often showing an idealized woman on skis with a skimpy fabric blowing in the breeze, while below a watchful man enjoys the spectacle. Men and women alike had to be "properly" dressed for the occasion. For early women skiers this involved an impractical woolen skirt; for men, fanciful tweeds and, of course, a fine tie.

The same adventurous spirit that drove the early skiing pioneers still remains with the skier of today. The thrill and exhilaration of participating in the sport of skiing certainly has not changed, although its visual portrayal has evolved considerably.

We can imagine what it would be like to be among the first pioneers to strap on a pair of hickory skis and begin our downhill descent... We can see ourselves in front of that jazzy new automobile at a glamorous ski resort... We can feel the winter sun...the excitement....

HISTORY OF SKIING

Rock wall carving from Rodoy, Norway. Man on skis. c.2500 B.C.

Early depiction of Scandinavian hunters on primitive skis.

Infant King Haakon Haakonson portrayed in 1853 painting, *Flight of the "Birchlegs"* (refers to the custom of wrapping legs with birch bark as protection against snow).

Skiing's Early Origins

Skiing, as a sport, is of comparatively recent origin. Skiing as a means of travel, however, existed from the time of man's earliest migrations. Physical evidence dates back to about 2500 B.C., and it includes a pair of preserved skis from central Sweden, and rock drawings from northern Norway showing a party of either hunters or warriors wearing skis. Literary reference to skiing can also be found in Europe's far north in Virgil's *Aeneid,* written almost 2000 years ago.

Throughout Nordic history, skiing has been a major catalyst of great events. An illustrative example is found in Swedish history. In 1521 the Danes overran Sweden and massacred all of the Swedish nobles but one, Gustav Vasa, who was able to escape. The Swedes were left without a leader, so two desperate peasants set out on skis to find Gustav. He came back, drove the Danes out of Sweden, and set up the kingdom of Sweden that survives to this day.

The role of skiing, in the rescue of Gustav Vasa during the Swedish Wars of Independence, and in a very similar account from Norway's Civil War involving the rescue of the infant King Haakon Haakonson in 1206, has become an important part of the national heritage of those countries.

The Swedes learned an invaluable lesson from the rescue of Gustav Vasa: the importance of skis in warfare. During the many wars of the sixteenth and seventeenth centuries, they equipped all of their winter troops with either skis or snowshoes. In the war of 1521, the Swedes stretched animal skins between two skis to carry injured comrades off the fields, and thus they created the first known stretchers.

In 1721 a ski company was organized within the Norwegian army. Twelve years later regular ski drills were held as part of maneuvers. The soldiers of this unit are generally credited with being the first to use a leather strap around their heel, in addition to the original toestrap, to keep their skis from falling off when skiing downhill. But even these bindings were too loose to permit full control of their skis, so a single solid pole was employed as a brake when skiing downhill and as a "pusher" to increase speed on flat surfaces.

By and large, early skiing was a utilitarian activity in the cold snowy regions of Scandinavia, offering practical transportation that would otherwise be impossible for armies, hunters and individuals. One journal describes the importance of skis to the woodsmen of Norway as "necessary to them in pursuing their labors as ordinary shoes are to inhabitants of cities."

The early Norwegian chronicler Paul B. Du Chaillu, in his *Land of the Midnight Sun,* gave a typical account of the mystique skiing held in the 1870s: "I have often trembled at seeing Norwegians or Lapps come down the mountains. The natives can easily go ten or fifteen miles an hour when the snow is firm and in good condition."

To arctic explorers, the "snowshoes" of Norway were indispensible for rugged adventures across the northern regions of Greenland. In describing his forthcoming expedition to find the northern terminus of Greenland, Lieutenant Robert E. Peary wrote: "It is the first attempt to reach a high latitude in Greenland overland, and will be the first American expedition to use the Norwegian snowshoe, or skate, which I found so invaluable in my preliminary reconnoissance of the Greenland 'inland ice' in 1886." Years later, Peary was credited with being the first person to reach the North Pole. Of course, he could not have accomplished his feats without the use of snowshoes, or skis.

The Evolution of Skiing As a Sport

Competitive skiing in Europe began in 1866 in Christiania (now known as Oslo), Norway with annual jumping and racing competitions. The skis employed were the traditional, basic transportation versions used by the Norwegians for centuries.

A Lapp going downhill on "snowshoes." 1879.

In 1868, Sondre Nordheim began experimenting with new ski designs in the Telemark district of Norway. Nordheim perfected a ski which, except in detail, was similiar to a modern downhill ski, lacking only a central groove and modern metal bindings. This was the first serious attempt to depart from the traditional pattern. With this experimental ski and a redesigned binding with heel and instep strap, Nordheim was able to revolutionize downhill running. Until then, it had been confined to straight running with occasional laborious turns, mainly achieved by stepping round. Braking was carried out by means of a long stout ski pole held across the body and pressed into the snow.

Telemark turn. 1923.

The young men of Telemark were performing extraordinary feats of jumping and downhill running with Sondre Nordheim's new skis, all a result of the control the new bindings gave them and the turning ability of the ski design. For the first time skiers were able to perform a series of linked "S" turns on steep slopes without any aid from their ski pole. They had invented what was subsequently known as the "telemark turn." Nordheim and his friends dominated every competition held in Christiania in 1868, the first year of the experimental skis. The following year, the competing Christiania boys answered with their own improved style. The long pole was discarded, and the upright position of jumping and running was adopted. They added a new turn which came to be known as the christiania. Techniques improved, competition was stiff, and the era of skiing as a sport was under way.

Norwegian travelers and emigrants quickly spread the virtues of this new sport throughout the world. In 1870 Norwegian gold miners climbed Mount Kosciusko in Australia on skis. By the end of the century there were skiers on nearly every continent of the world. Nordheim himself emigrated to the United States in 1883 and became a leading spirit of skiing in this country.

The Spread of Skiing Throughout Europe

Controlling downhill speed by "braking." Australia. c.1905.

In 1888, a major catalyst began influencing a change in skiing from an obscure pastime of Norwegians and immigrants to a popular international sport. It was in this year that the Norwegian scientist Fridtjof Nansen crossed the continent of Greenland on skis and wrote of his experiences two years later in a book which became an overnight best-seller: *The First Crossing of Greenland.* Nansen describes the great spiritual and physical pleasure derived from skiing:

> *"Where will one find more freedom and excitement than when gliding swiftly down the hillsides through woods, your cheeks brushed by the sharp cold air and frosted pine branches — with eye, brain and muscles alert and prepared to meet every unknown obstacle and danger which the next instant may throw in one's path? Does it not feel as though the mind is suddenly cleansed of a trying civilization and smokey city air?"*

Fridtjof Nansen, who crossed Greenland on skis. 1888.

Nansen's book fired the imagination of adventurous people around the world, who then quickly took to the "new" sport of skiing for pleasure.

A young Austrian military officer, Mathias Zdarsky, was introduced to skiing through Nansen's book, and he practiced in the Black Forest of Germany. He was quick to realize the potential for skis to assist the Imperial Austrian Army in patrolling a long and very mountainous frontier, provided that a safe and simple method could be devised to master the steep slopes. For six years Zdarsky perfected the technique now known as the stem-christiania. It was the "stem-christie" that enabled the skier to descend slopes of any steepness in a series of S-turns, regardless of snow consistency. Zdarsky set up an Army ski school in Lillienfeld near Vienna in 1896 which attracted skiers from all over central Europe. The Lillienfeld ski school was the first organized and planned system for teaching people to ski.

Zdarsky's technique was based on using a long pole both to balance and to brake. The skis were very short (five feet) and wide (four inches), which made turning easy on the steep slopes. Later, Zdarsky started using two poles, widened the stem, and developed the snowplow. Zdarsky is known to many as "the father of alpine skiing." However, Zdarsky maintained that the sport of the time was the climb, not the downhill rush, and his technique failed to progress beyond the early success it had achieved. There was intense interest and controversy over various other methods of the time.

The English also read of Nansen. Early British skiers imported Norwegian skis and traveled to the Swiss resorts of Davos, Grindelwald, Adelboden and throughout the Alps. They introduced holiday skiing to these resorts and, during the 1890s and early 1900s, exercised a controlling influence on the sport, especially after the creation of the Ski Club of Great Britain in 1903. It was Englishmen from the Ski Club of Great Britain who modernized Zdarsky's Alpine method. This technique offered easier ways to turn by analyzing the physical forces involved in skiing movements. The braking stick was discarded from skiing forever.

It was during this pre-World War I period that skiing first came to be viewed by many as a glamour sport. It was seen as a sport for the adventurous and wealthy, who had both time and money to travel from Britain to the Alps.

While Zdarsky may have been the first prominent instructor, another Austrian, Hannes Schneider became the most influential. Before Schneider's arrival, much of

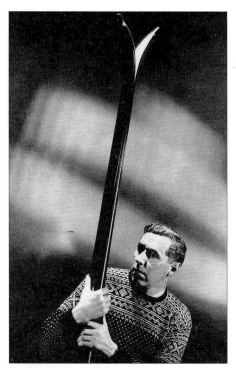

Hannes Schneider. 1936.

sport skiing was regarded as a method of getting up a mountain rather than down. Schneider was the primary influence in transforming skiing from a means to an end. To Hannes Schneider, controlled speed was the attraction in skiing, so he developed the Arlberg technique during World War I for skiing down steep, icy slopes. This technique utilized a crouch which lowered the center of gravity. When skiing for the beginner became popular, the Arlberg system was employed as the convenient method for teaching skiing.

The International Federation of Skiing was revived in 1922 and was responsible for the organization of the first Winter Olympics, held in Chamonix, France in 1924. Initially, the competition was entirely Nordic (cross-country). It was not until the Olympic Games of 1932 in Lake Placid, New York that Alpine events, including slalom and downhill, were added.

By the 1930s there was much information and activity available to the adventurous skier: books, ski journals, quality ski equipment, highly-refined ski instruction, destination ski areas, ski clubs and associations, and travel programs. Basic transportation for Scandinavians had now become a recreational pastime for people all over the world.

American Skiing Origins

With the strong Scandinavian tradition of skiing, it is no surprise that it was Scandinavian immigrants who brought skiing to the United States. From the pioneer Midwest, through the camps strung along the high rib of the Continental Divide, and to the high country of Colorado, Utah and California, early Norwegian settlers spread their enthusiasm for skiing across the U.S. They used their skis for winter transportation, much like they had done at home.

Rev. John L. Dyer was an itinerant Methodist preacher who went west to Colorado in the early 1850s. He wrote of his experiences during the winter of 1861-62 and described his skis, which at that time were called "snowshoes." "My snowshoes were of Norway style, from nine to eleven feet in length, and ran well when the snow was just right, but very heavy when they gathered snow. I carried a pole to jar the sticking snow off."

But the Reverand Dyer was not the only one who skied in the days of the hard-drinking, rugged mining camps of the early 1850s. There were many pioneers on skis who helped bring about the opening of the new American West. The most famous was a man who became a legend and was known as "Snowshoe" Thompson. In 1851 John A. Thompson left his small village north of Oslo, Norway and moved to California to join the gold rush. Once there, Thompson realized there was more money to be made in supplying the miners with services than there was in mining itself. During the harsh winters, the settlers in the rich valleys at the eastern base of the high Sierras of California were unable to receive mail or any communications, due to the frequent storms which often left snow to depths of fifteen or twenty feet. Fearless men attempted again and again to scale the snow-crowned summits in order to carry the mail to these inland-bound people, but often sacrificed their lives to their temerity.

"Snowshoe" Thompson, on "snow skates," carrying the mails in the California Sierra. 1856.

The hearty Norwegian, Thompson, proposed to carry mail to these people through the winter, on what were then called "snow-skates." His proposition was received with much incredulity at first, but he soon proved that he was in earnest. He had been trained from boyhood in his native land of Norway to use snow-skates, and he soon manufactured a pair of skis according to his early recollections of Norwegian ones.

In January of 1856 Thompson strapped a mailbag on his back and went from Placerville to Carson Valley, a distance of ninety miles, using twenty-five-pound oak skis. After successfully completing this trip, "Snowshoe" Thompson became a necessity to the miners in the Sierra for many years to come. His travels provided the only land communication between the Atlantic coastal states and California during the winters of the early 1860s. "Snowshoe's" exploits on skis became the topic of folklore for generations to come.

Map route of "Snowshoe" Thompson.

Meanwhile, the use of "Norwegian snowshoes" spread throughout the Sierra mining camps. The Sierra winters were very long, and the mining camp amusements, aside from drinking and an occasional fistfight, were few. To break the monotony, someone came up with the bright idea of holding "snowshoe races." This was not transportation; this was downhill sport.

The first matchups, held about 1860, were informal affairs. Soon the races became major events which were hotly contested. The various mining camps organized teams and challenged each other on courses that went straight down open Sierra mountainsides lined with hundreds of wagering spectators.

La Porte, California was both a commercial center of the mining district and the hub of snowshoe racing. By 1867 racing had become so popular that La Porte skiers organized the Alturas Snowshoe Club, which formalized racing rules, sponsored tournaments, and was one of the world's first ski associations. With the end of the gold boom, mining camps faded and snowshoe racing in the California Sierra appeared to die away forever.

La Porte, California, USA. c.1905.

Then, in the 1880s skiing again took on a sporting component when Scandinavian immigrants such as Sondre Nordheim introduced ski jumping to the northern areas of Michigan, Wisconsin, Minnesota and New England; places where skiing later grew into a popular spectator sport.

After early California experiences in the Sierra and competitions among emigrants in the Midwest and New England, there were few gains in participant popularity. This was largely due to the fact that there were no ski handbooks, no instructors, and knowledge of skiing was spread only by word-of-mouth. Equipment was scarce, exceedingly rustic, and primitive.

Skiing as an Organized Sport in America

One of the first organized ski meets in America was a jumping contest held in 1888 in Ishpeming, a town in Upper Michigan's iron-mining country. Ishpeming boasted a ski club whose purpose was to promote jumping and to organize competitions. In 1904 some members of the club were determined to conduct formal tournaments and to set standards that participating clubs could follow. The newly-founded organization was called the National Ski Association of America.

The National Ski Association began to standardize competition primarily in the Midwest and later throughout the entire nation as more and more clubs joined its ranks. The Association attracted affiliate divisions throughout the country, eventually becoming the United States Ski Association, which is the current governing body of competitive skiing in the U.S.

In contrast to the National Ski Association, which flourished in the Midwest in a formalized, professional tradition, east coast skiing began as a sport for the amateur. Skiing in the east was for the most part under the dominion of the colleges and universities.

Early ski jumping competition. 1905.

Fred H. Harris was an influential person in organizing skiing on the east coast. He learned to ski as a sophomore in high school and then went to Dartmouth College in Hanover, New Hampshire. In 1910, Harris decided to form an organized club for ski and winter outings, and he called it The Dartmouth Outing Club. His motive was to "escape the tedium of winter behind bolts."

The Dartmouth Outing Club was an innovative influence in the history of skiing. The Club originated The Winter Carnival and sponsored the first intercollegiate skiing tournaments. They also recruited a ski coach in 1923 who was a pupil of Mathias Zdarsky, thus beginning the tradition of importing European ski coaches and instructors to the United States. One of the Club founders went on to institute one of the first snow trains.

Another hired Otto Schniebs, the man who brought the Arlberg Ski Technique to America. The United States Eastern Amateur Ski Association was also the brainchild of Fred Harris and the Dartmouth Outing Club.

The Dartmouth Outing Club was at the forefront in establishing Alpine (downhill) ski competition in the United States, and it contributed immeasurably to the great growth and popularity of skiing nationwide.

Dartmouth Winter Carnival. c.1935.

Ski Equipment and Clothing

Early versions of skis tended to be hand fashioned by Scandinavian immigrants in the same manner as in the old country. The first ski factory was not established in the U.S. until 1888, and with only a few exceptions, it was not until the 1920s that production skis were available in quantities from several American manufacturers. Some patient skiers ordered their equipment from English or Scandinavian winter sports catalogs.

The California Sierra skiers of a century ago no doubt attired themselves in whatever clothes happened to be handy. Prior to about 1930, skiers wore strictly functional outdoor clothing that was seldom designed specifically for skiing. They favored standard workshirts and high boots covered with gaiters. In some photos, it appears that a few are wearing the original model of Levi jeans. Though they tended to restrict movement, woolen hunting clothes were popular, as were knickers, and in some cases, riding breeches. Knickers provided more freedom of movement, al-

Women's fashions. 1916.

Fashionable men's dress. c.1910.

Symphony conductor Leopold Stowkowski and movie star Sie Holmquist, the "Mary Pickford of Sweden." Lake Placid. 1921.

though the neckties sometimes worn along with them certainly did not.

Women had few options at the beginning. Long, heavy skirts were apparently mandatory skiwear as late as the beginning of this century. The skirts may have preserved one's modesty (except perhaps during a fall), but they were not very functional.

The early 1930s saw the first American clothing designed specifically for skiing. At first, these styles tended to be baggy (for movement) and woolen (for warmth). Ski parkas also appeared about this time. Many styles were brought to this country by ski instructors from Europe, where ski fashions were somewhat more advanced.

America's First Winter Resort

Lake Placid set the scene for what was soon to revolutionize skiing forever. The Lake Placid Club was a fashionable summer sporting club and resort in a little village in upstate New York. During the winter of 1904-5, the Club decided to stay open for the winter season, offering ice skating, tobogganing and skiing, thus becoming the first continuously operating ski and winter sports resort in America. Its opening and its success heralded the birth of commercialized skiing in this country. Lake Placid became the leading winter sports center of the United States before World War I. Its ever-expanding facilities brought the III Olympic Winter Games to the resort in 1932. The sport of skiing was coming of age.

In the United States, the most far-reaching result of the 1932 Winter Olympics was the wave of interest and enthusiasm generated for winter sports, especially for skiing. The media loved portraying the sport in splashy, decorative displays, often with accompanying photos of the many political, film and sports notables who were spectators or participants in the increasingly popular sport.

The First Uphill Tows

After almost a century of climbing uphill, it took the inventive genius of a skier to come up with a mechanical device that would propel skiers back up the hill, if not effortlessly, then at least faster and less laboriously than had ever been possible before. It was simple, like so many great inventions, but it worked, and it changed the whole course of the sport's history overnight. It was called a rope tow. While there had been many other attempts at uphill conveyance since the turn of the century, including cable cars and railcars, none were as practical as the easy-to-operate and simple-to-use rope tow.

The first patent on record was issued in 1932 to a young Swiss engineer. Later that year the first rope tow in North America appeared on Foster's Hill at Shawbridge, Canada, in the Laurentians. It was an old Dodge chassis, a series of pulleys and wheels, and a rope spliced head to tail, running endlessly for skiers to hold for their ride up the hill. In 1934, offering a tow cost of $1 a day, the first U.S. version appeared in Woodstock, Vermont on Gilbert's Hill, which became the Kitty Hawk of the American ski scene. With cheap, fairly reliable methods for uphill transportation available, rope tows spread rapidly to every part of the country.

In the middle 1930s the slopes were alive from coast to coast, with many new skiers enjoying recently installed rope tows. In 1935 eastern U.S. railroads began offering the clever idea of "snow trains" from major urban areas to ski destinations. Initial departures were from New York, Boston and other eastern cities, with later routes from Chicago, San Francisco, Seattle and other major points in the midwest and west. The snow trains offered live entertainment, dancing and libations to encourage a lively time for all. The destination resorts made rapid advancements to try to keep up with the increased demands from snow train arrivals, but they were unable to provide adequate facilities to support the needs of people traveling a great time and distance.

America's first rope tow at Woodstock Ski Hill, Woodstock, Vermont. 1935.

Sun Valley — America's First World Class Ski Resort

In 1932, at the age of forty, W. Averell Harriman stepped in as board chairman of his family's Union Pacific Railroad. While the Union Pacific railroad cars became modern and progressive, other Western railroads had more awe-inspiring destinations than the Union Pacific. The Santa Fe had the Grand Canyon and made much of it. The Southern Pacific had lavish Palm Springs, and the Canadian Pacific had Lake Louise and Banff. The Union Pacific needed an exclusive attraction — a glamorous location to pull in customers.

Snow trains unloading skiers at the slopes. 1930's.

Harriman became convinced that traditional summer resorts were a thing of the past, while the great winter sport centers like St. Moritz, Switzerland were thriving. He could not help but notice that after the 1932 Olympics at Lake Placid, New York, skiing in the U.S. was beginning to boom.

In 1935 Harriman dreamed about an American ski and winter sports center somewhere in the vast empire of the western United States. Properly developed, he believed such a place would be patronized annually by thousands of Americans and would rival famous European snow resorts in the Swiss, French, Austrian and Italian Alps.

An Austrian friend of Harriman's, Count Felix Schaffgotsch, was hired and set out in November of 1935 to find the perfect mountain resort location in the United States. He was looking for dry powder snow and sunshine. He also wanted wide-open slopes, because Easterners were having a miserable time skiing down old, narrow logging roads. He wanted wooded hills in the background to provide a scenic effect.

A test of optimum loading speed for Sun Valley's first ski season. 1936.

The Count traveled to Mount Rainier in Washington, Mount Hood in Oregon, Lake Tahoe, Yosemite National Park, and the San Bernardino Mountains in California, Zion National Park, Alta and Brighton in Utah, Rocky Mountain National Park and Berthoud Pass in Colorado, and Jackson Hole, Wyoming, but he was not completely satisfied with these locations as prospective resorts. Finally, his search ended in central Idaho near an old mining town called Ketchum. Harriman and the Count deemed this the "ideal" location for a world-class winter resort.

Work on the resort began in June, 1936. Publicist Steve Hannagan named the beautiful location "Sun Valley" to dispel the myth that wintertime must be harsh and cold. Hannagan insisted that there be some sort of device to get the skiers to the top of the mountain. In the east, rope tows and "J" bars were being used. But Hannagan

Advertisement of Sun Valley's first ski season. 1936.

did not think that mode of transportation was dignified enough for the distinguished guests of Sun Valley.

The engineers at Union Pacific's headquarters went to work. One of them remembered a mono-cable-tram device used in Venezuela to bring huge bunches of bananas from the mountaintops down to the freighters waiting on the docks. The engineers replaced the hook with a chair, and...voila! The first two chairlifts in the world were operable for the resort's grand opening in December, 1936.

The opening of Sun Valley in 1936 heralded the present-day era of skiing. This new era was characterized by luxury accommodations, superb dining, heated swimming pools, ice skating rinks, unique chair lifts, European ski instructors, and fun ski trains to take skiers to their destinations painlessly. The media brought the public's attention to film celebrities on skis and thus to the newly emerging glamorous sport of skiing.

The Sun Valley Lodge. 1936.

Magazines across America began to feature skiing images on their covers to attract readers to the exciting "new sport." Advertisers rapidly increased their use of skiing as a theme to sell products of all types. Publishers began to mass-produce commercial post cards. The rush to contemporary skiing was on... A new era had begun.

Conclusion

The development of the Sun Valley ski resort brings us to the end of the era of early skiing from 1856 to 1936. From "Snowshoe" Thompson to Sun Valley. From Norway to America. From a sport of survival to one of luxury. From rugged mountaineering to modern chair lifts. From primitive snowshoes to technologically advanced ski equipment. It was an exciting eighty years, dramatic in its evolution as portrayed in the graphics and illustrations presented in this volume.

Life. L.T. Holton. 1927.

HISTORY OF THE ILLUSTRATED MAGAZINE

"A *work of art cannot be satisfied with being a representation; it should be a presentation."*

Jacques Reverdy
French artist, twentieth century

The meeting of Mr. Jackson and Fridtjof Nansen in Greenland. *The Illustrated London News.* 1896.

The first magazines were published in France in 1665. Others soon followed around the world, and they were typical of the visually dry and textually dull publications that appeared during the first 200 years of magazine history. Most publishers did not realize the significance of visuals as tools to educate, shape opinions, entertain, and sell greater numbers of their magazines.

It was only during the mid-nineteenth century that the magazine changed from an elitist publication to the main source of popular entertainment for the general public. Instead of speaking primarily to the well-educated upper classes, the magazine addressed a broad cross section of the population. Aided and inspired by the cultural and technical changes resulting from the Industrial Revolution, the new, modern magazine enjoyed a meteoric rise in popularity in Europe, the United States and elsewhere. By 1890 it had begun its most colorful period.

It was through the addition of illustration that the periodical found its new character and vitality in the Victorian Age. With the emergence of the magazine, art was disseminated to substantial numbers of people for the first time in history.

Until that time all art forms had been relatively inaccessible to the general public, remaining in the hands of privileged friends and patrons of the artists or publicly displayed in faraway cities. The same inaccessibility was true of the sport of skiing. As the public's appreciation of art grew, the magazine proved to be an important stage for artists of all persuasions to depict skiing in all of its romantic glory.

The magazine cover, like the magazine itself, had been neglected as a decorative element in its early years. But with the increase in vivid dramatic illustrations came the discovery that the magazine cover had important powers to influence and amuse.

It was Great Britain that took the early lead in producing illustrated periodicals during the nineteenth century. Publishers, as well as master engravers and artists, sensed the public's readiness to spend a shilling a copy to enjoy the latest illustrations, which were often eyewitness accounts of current events.

There are two apparent reasons for the emergence of Great Britain as the early leader of illustrated periodicals and books: its efficient communications system for distribution of publications and its educated public to read them. However, other countries soon began to catch up with and eventually surpass Great Britain in the visual arts.

With the emergence of *Frank Leslie's Illustrated Weekly* and *Harper's Weekly,* the modern illustrated periodical was born in America. It took American marketing ingenuity to become the link that propelled the magazine into the hands of vast numbers of people.

The late nineteenth century was a time of great social change during which traditional class structures were being eroded. Magazines were an important focus for people as they experienced a shifting of social values. Skiing was brought to light through accounts and illustrations of early arctic explorers, travelers visiting faraway Norway and early pioneers in the American West.

Munsey's Magazine. 1908.

Perhaps the 1890s should have been called the "more decade" — more money, more leisure, education, sports and entertainment. As explorers and travelers rediscovered skiing, it followed that the sport of skiing would be extensively offered to the magazine public.

Production of magazines went through revolutionary changes by the late nineteenth century. Until that time, it was a difficult, time-consuming and costly task to produce the visuals accompanying magazine text. Publications would often share the $300 to $500 cost for a full-page woodcut with other publishers. This prohibitive cost was reduced as technological changes made economies of scale possible.

A typical magazine illustration took three weeks to complete in the mid-nineteenth century. By 1872 the process of making an illustration from start to finish took one week. Ten years later it had been refined to two days, and by 1900 shortened to a few hours. Photoengraving came into use about this time, radically reducing the time and cost for producing magazine graphics. It reduced a long, laborious process to a simple, mechanical one.

In addition to photography, the other important technical advancement for magazine illustration was the color revolution. Color lithography enabled magazines to display beautiful works of art with a quality never dreamed possible by most people. The color revolution produced intensified public interest in prints, posters and magazine covers. As a result, important artists such as Will Bradley, Edward Penfield, Charles Dana Gibson and Maxfield Parrish were drawn to these media. Other famous illustrators included Harrison Fisher (The Fisher Girl), Howard Chandler Christy (Christy Girls), Jessie Wilcox Smith (wide-eyed children), and Norman Rockwell (all-American scenes).

Cavalry officers inspecting Yellowstone Park in winter. *Harper's Weekly.* Frederic Remington. 1898.

Magazines used vivid illustrations to attract readers, showing the Norwegian sport of "snowshoeing," the "exotic daredevils" of ski jumping, and the runners going "a mile a minute" down steep slopes in the mining camps.

Looking at magazine covers, one can understand the important interaction between the magazine and fine art. Clearly, the magazine, and its cover in particular, comprised an important medium allowing many remarkable artists to test their artistic and experimental works in public. The cover also became a medium through which fine art was diffused into a more commercial form, more readily available to the masses.

During the early decades of the twentieth century, the magazine industry flourished. Since radio generally did not enter American households until the early 1920s, magazines enjoyed a captive market. There were fears, of course, that the popularity of radio would completely smother the magazine industry. Fortunately, it did not.

One of the keys to the success of magazine publishing was the increase in advertising, which helped lower the public price of each magazine and, in turn, boosted circulation. Advertisers pumped large sums of money into the industry, as they discovered that the buying power of the rising middle class could best be tapped through magazines.

The biggest effect on the magazine industry in the 1930s was not the Depression or international political tension, but the publication of *Life* magazine in 1936. With 96 pages of photographs and only a minimum of text, *Life* brought photo-journalism into unprecedented importance, as the photographer took the magazine cover away from the illustrator.

Ironically, it was one of the first issues of *Life* which featured a photographic account of the 1936 opening of Sun Valley, signaling the beginning of the end to a dramatic and wonderful period of magazine illustration, as well as bringing forth a new awareness of modern skiing.

Life features opening of Sun Valley. 1937.

Bear hunting in Sweden.
The Illustrated London News. 1856.

Sport in Lapland: A wolf hunt on "ski."
The Graphic. W.T. Maud. 1900.

"Snowshoe" racing in the mountains of
California [world's first illustration of a ski race].
Pacific Rural Press. 1874.

"Snowshoe" jumping in Norway.
The Graphic. 1883.

THE GRAPHIC

AN ILLUSTRATED WEEKLY NEWSPAPER

No. 1,398—Vol. LIV. | Registered as a Newspaper · · · · · SATURDAY, SEPTEMBER 12, 1896 WITH EXTRA FOUR-PAGE SUPPLEMENT *"The Riots in Constantinople"* · · · · PRICE SIXPENCE By Post 6½d.

Mr. Harry Fisher, the botanist of the Jackson Expedition, who has returned home in the *Windward*, thus describes Dr. Nansen's appearance when met by Mr. Jackson on the ice near Cape Flora :—" Now we had time to look at Nansen, and it is certain his nearest relation would not have recognised him. He was absolutely black from head to foot. His light hair and moustache were jet black, and there was not a speck of white about his face or hands. He looked for all the world like a nigger, and the brightness of his eyes was accentuated by the grime of his face, which had been blackened by the blubber-smoke. His clothes—the one suit he had worn for fifteen months—were stiff with blood and oil with which his face and hands were also covered." As soon as ever the first greetings were over, Dr. Nansen and Lieutenant Johansen enjoyed what was to them a great luxury, namely, a good wash

DR. NANSEN AS HE APPEARED WHEN MET BY MR. JACKSON IN FRANZ JOSEF LAND

From a Photograph taken by Mr. Jackson on their arrival at Elmwood

Fridtjof Nansen on his expedition crossing
Greenland. *The Graphic.* 1896.

Lieutenant Robert E. Peary, U.S.N. preparing for
Arctic expedition.
Harper's Weekly. W.A. Rogers. 1891.

Lieutenant Peary and his companion, Domn
Gracle of Sweden.
Harper's Weekly. W.A. Rogers. 1891.

On "Norwegian Shoes" in Middle Park, Colorado.
Frank Leslie's Illustrated Newspaper. 1877.

"Snowshoeing" in Yellowstone.
Harper's Weekly. Charles Graham. 1887.

SKEE-RUNNING ON THE SNOW-COVERED HILLS OF OREGON.
DRAWN FROM LIFE BY W. A. ROGERS.—[SEE PAGE 225.]

Harper's Weekly. W.A. Rogers. 1899.

The Graphic. H. Reuterdahl. 1893.

Norwegian sport at Ishpeming, Michigan.
Harper's Weekly. Thulstrup and Graham. 1892.

Norwegian "ski" or snowshoe racing, near
Christiania.
The Illustrated London News. 1894.

Collier's Weekly. 1902.

A race on "skees."
The Youth's Companion. 1902.

The Graphic. 1894

Increasing the speed of "ski-running."
The Illustrated London News. W. Russell Flint.
1906.

Boy's Companion. 1915.

Collier's

THE NATIONAL WEEKLY

THE CRISIS IN RUSSIA

Photographs of the Czar, his Bodyguard, and Street Scenes in St. Petersburg

Vol XXXIV No 19   FEBRUARY 4 1905   PRICE 10 CENTS

Collier's. Steele. 1905.

Harper's Weekly. Rollin McNeil Crampton. 1910.

The Pittsburg Dispatch. A.G. Hull. 1912.

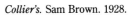

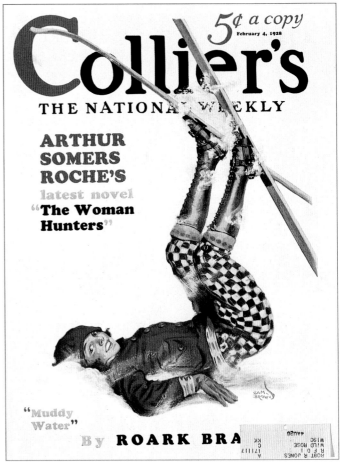

Judge. Delevaute. 1927.

Collier's. Sam Brown. 1928.

The Lost Ski [President William Taft].
Puck Magazine. Joseph Keppler. 1911.

Woman's Home Companion. 1907.

Country Life. Edwin R. Wilson. 1920.

The American Legion Weekly.
Emmett Watson. 1923.

Modern Priscilla. Marguerite Davis. 1922.

The Saturday Evening Post. Eugene Ivory. 1928.

Judge. Eugene Gise. 1928.

Judge. Holmgren. 1931.

WOMAN'S WORLD

FEBRUARY · 1929   *"Sports of 1929!"*   10 CENTS A COPY

THE NEW SPRING FASHIONS · EXCLUSIVE STYLE NOTES FROM PARIS
Features by—Dean Heffernan · James Oppenheim · Dana Gatlin · Morris Fishbein, M.D.
STUNNING NEEDLEWORK NOVELTIES FOR THE MODERN WOMAN

Woman's World. Miriam Story Hurford. 1929.

Pictorial Review. McClelland Barclay. 1929.

Ladies' Home Journal. Hayden Hayden. 1929.

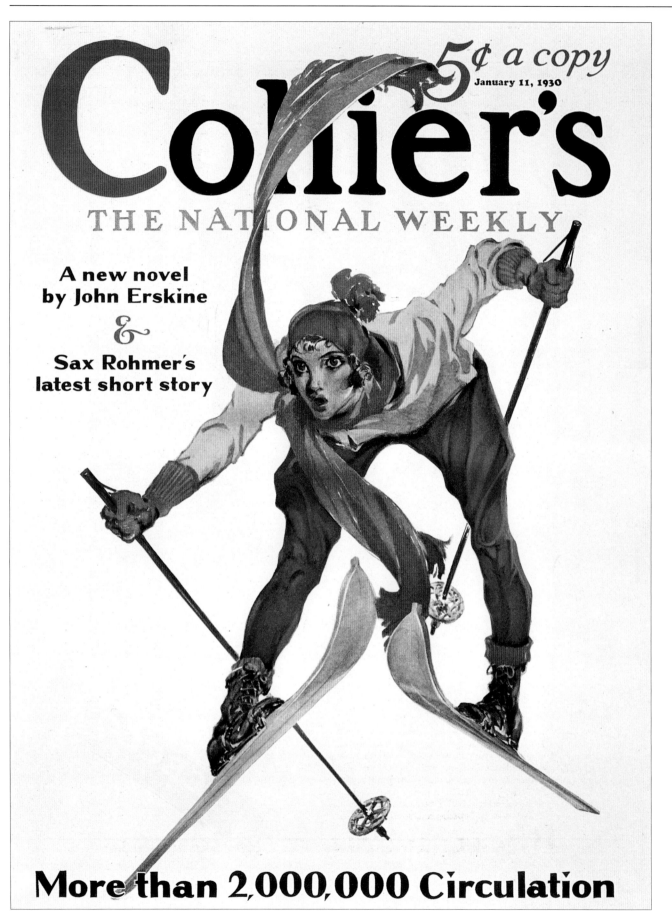

Collier's. 1930.

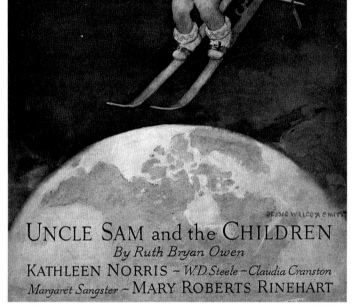

Good Housekeeping.
Jessie Wilcox Smith. 1931.

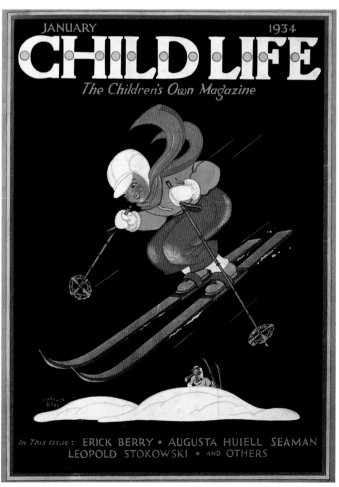

Child Life. Clarence Biers. 1934.

Ladies' Home Journal. Maxfield Parrish. 1931.

The Saturday Evening Post. James McKell. 1931.

Judge. Johan Bull. 1932.

The New Yorker. Perry Barlow. 1935.

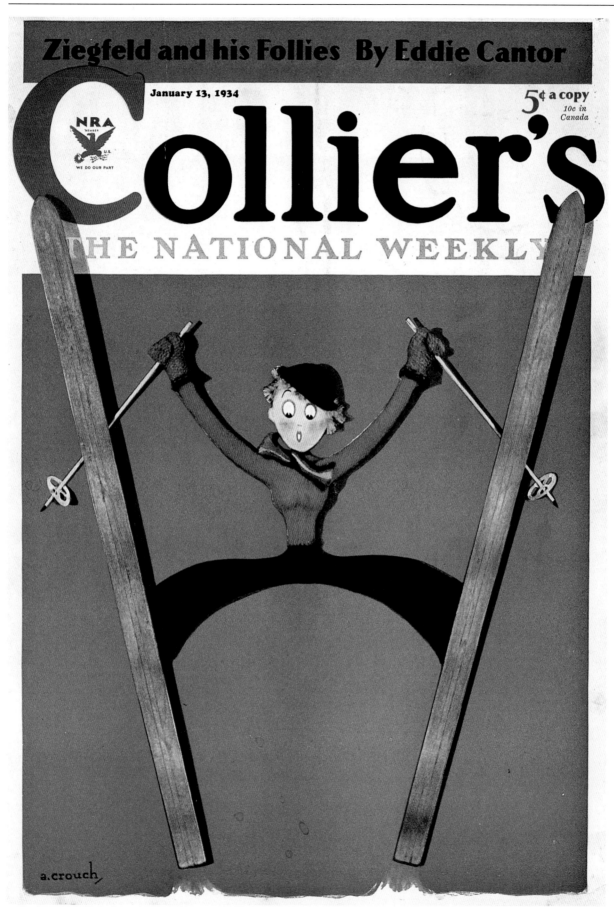

Collier's. Arthur Crouch. 1934.

The American Magazine. John LaGatta. 1933.

Country Gentleman. Carolyn Haywood. 1934.

Judge. Vernon Grant. 1935.

Collier's. Arthur Crouch. 1935.

Collier's. Arthur Crouch. 1936.

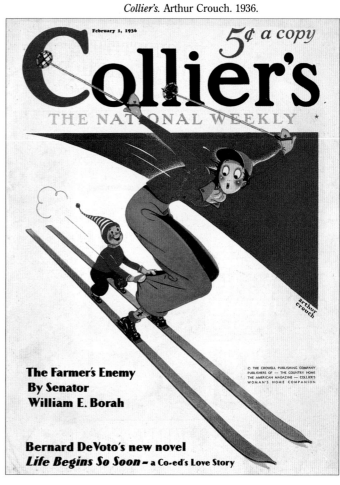

Harper's Bazaar. Erte. 1935.

Vogue. Benito. 1931.

Ladies' Home Journal. John LaGatta. 1934.

The American Legion Monthly. Tenggren. 1933.

Ladies' Home Journal. 1935.

The Saturday Evening Post.
Bradshaw Crandell. 1935.

Pictorial Review. 1934.

Collier's. Mario Cooper. 1935.

Vanity Fair. 1936.

The Coca-Cola Company. 1922.

HISTORY OF ADVERTISING ILLUSTRATION

*"**A**dvertising is now so near to perfection that it is not easy to propose any improvement."*

Samuel Johnson
Author, 1759

Matterhorn Alpine Ski. 1905.

In spite of Dr. Johnson's prophesy more than two centuries ago, advertising has indeed seen vast changes and improvements. It has evolved into a major cultural part of our society today, with U.S. advertisers spending well over $50 billion a year to promote and sell their goods and services.

Advertising, destined to be the omnipresent, most characteristic and most remunerative form of American literature, did not come into its own until the second half of the nineteenth century.

Prior to the U.S. Civil War, with the factory system still in its infancy, agriculture was the dominant source of national wealth. The market for the products of these early manufacturing and agricultural enterprises was generally the people living in the village, town or city immediately surrounding the producing center.

A fledgling distribution network existed to carry these products to other markets (there were more than 30,000 rail miles in the U.S. in 1860), but there was little demand for its use other than for agricultural products. At this early stage in American manufacturing, sophisticated distribution of goods was not yet developed.

In a selling environment, in which producers were assured of a larger market than their productive capacities could meet, it is not surprising to find that most manufacturers did not attempt to differentiate their own product from similiar goods. Their products usually carried no identifying brands or marks, and they were normally sold by local retailers from bulk lots, along with the products of other producers.

With the majority of producers thus enjoying an assured market, the small amount of advertising that was done during this pre-war period was placed by retailers attempting to reach customers in their stores' immediate geographic areas. The medium for carrying these factual-only notices was the local newspaper. Aside from printed notices and posters, this was the only practical choice available.

The U.S. Civil War accelerated a national trend towards industrialization, and for the first time there was some tentative use of advertising beyond the retail level. With the completion of the transcontinental railroad, the continental age of advertising had truly begun.

At the outset of the 1880s manufacturers were blessed by blossoming sales. They had just emerged from a decade that had seen the invention of the telephone, the incandescent lamp and significant innovations in factory products. In 1880 alone there were applications for more than 13,000 copyrights and patents, giving rise to an ever-increasing stream of new products from mills and factories.

The potential consumer markets for these goods were also increasing at a dramatic rate, expanding with the transportation capabilities provided by thousands of miles of railroads and roads throughout the ever-enlarging American nation.

In order to achieve effective distribution of their products, manufacturers needed an advertising medium that could reach all sections of their expanded market area. Such a medium was the national magazine, transported by the railroad lines into the American towns, where store shelves carried branded products brought by the same rails.

The increasingly popular tool of advertising in magazines led to some spectacular sales successes by its regular users. This success led to a further increase in advertising, which in turn helped lower the public price of each magazine and, as a result, boosted circulation. Advertisers pumped large sums of money into the industry, as they discovered that the buying power of the rising middle class could best be tapped through magazines. Thus, advertising was inextricably tied to the growth of newspapers, magazines and increased consumerism.

Advertising also changed the entire concept of magazine publishing. Up to this time publishers had generally relied on the readers themselves to pay for the cost of the magazines through the newsstand and subscription prices. But as advertising revenue continued to show the advertisers' confidence in the medium to economically deliver a selling message, this concept changed. So it was that in 1890 a publisher was quoted as saying, "If I can get a circulation of 400,000, I can afford to give my magazine away to anyone who'll pay the postage." The publisher was no longer simply creating a medium of entertainment, but rather a profitable advertising vehicle that would reach a certain number of potential customers to fully fund his magazine.

As advanced technology permitted low-cost reproduction of illustrations and color lithography, advertisers became increasingly competitive in their creativity. This led to new found uses of graphics in advertising, in order to give the reader a visual image of the product or to evoke a positive feeling towards the product.

It is not difficult to understand why the English Prime Minister, William Gladstone, insisted on sending to America for magazines, even when English editions were available. It was the American advertisements that fascinated him.

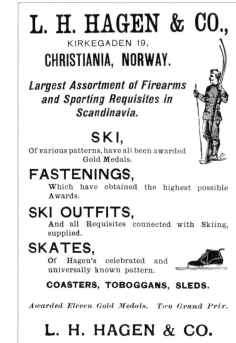

L.H. Hagen & Co. 1905.

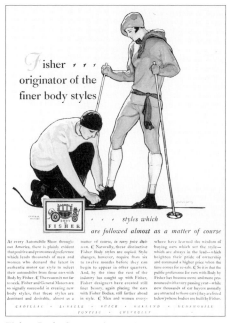

Fisher Body Corporation. 1925.

Skiing was associated with a life of leisure, adventure and good taste. Advertisers of many products incorporated these lifestyle images into their product messages through the use of skiing illustrations. The visual associations consumers made when seeing skiing graphics created great interest in the sport itself. As the public was hungrily trying new consumer products, they were equally enthusiastic to learn of the exciting and adventurous new sport from Norway.

By the 1920s and 1930s advertising art came into its own as never before in history. The new freedom allowed outstanding artists to use skiing to enrich the appeal of all useful objects. Manufacturers hired some of the best illustrators and artists to create the visual messages they desired.

The illustrations that follow are wonderful examples of the graphic advances used in advertising during skiing's early growth years. Through them you can enter a world where you can make ski jumps of 100 feet, ski in St. Moritz with your La Salle automobile, drive the latest model Studebaker or Packard to the slopes, or have snow-white teeth.

STYLE HAS BEEN SET TO SWIFTER TEMPO

. . . and none so fleet, so smart, so stalwart

as the new Studebakers!

The New President Eight Brougham for Five bespeaks eloquently the velvet road-mastery of its 115-horsepower world-champion chassis. Broadcloth upholstery of French pillow type, with folding center arm rest in rear seat, and adjustable driver's seat. Priced $2350, at the factory. Equipment, other than standard, extra.

The New President Eight Convertible Cabriolet for Four splendidly interprets the unmatched performance it provides. Folding top permits this smart closed car to be converted into an open roadster. Dual carburetion. Houdaille double-acting hydraulic shock absorbers. Priced $1895, at the factory. Equipment, other than standard, extra.

JUST as a musician weaves the pattern of his theme in rhythmic harmony, so have Studebaker's artists in coachcraft expressed the brilliant spirit of these new champion motor cars.

Fleetness, stamina and trustworthiness — far beyond what other motor cars have ever proved — are the qualities which enable Studebaker to hold *every* official stock car speed and endurance record. And these are the very attributes interpreted in every virile line and contour of these incomparable new Studebakers!

Studebaker. 1929.

Mellin's Food Company. 1899.

E. Howard Watch Company
[Robert E. Peary]. 1908.

Folmer Graflex Corporation. 1928.

Ansco Company. 1915.

There's Only One Camera
for such action

GRAFLEX

It's the one camera that shows you, definitely, in advance, exactly what the composition and focus of the final picture will be. · · · · · ·

And now there's a Graflex priced within reach of everybody. "Series B"—3¼" x 4¼"—speed up to 1/1000 second—$80—other models $85 to $375.

Featured by A Good Dealer Everywhere

FOLMER GRAFLEX CORP. ROCHESTER, NEW YORK

The new Packard Imperial Limousine, seven passengers

Why do men ski?

In free flight—down the long incline he sweeps at the speed of the wind.

Not hampered is he by that resisting force—*vibration*.

Slivers of wood and flakes of snow furnish him the simple means of obtaining the thrilling sense of unfettered power.

Smoothest speed is not only desirable from the standpoint of pleasure—but it is always most *efficient speed*.

Because the Twin Six engine has minimized vibration—it not only adds to the exhilarating joy of motoring—but conserves the stored-up power of gasoline.

Twelve balanced and sprightly cylinders divide the stresses of the load—and give to this newest Packard great, smooth, *economical* power.

And now—we must save gasoline.

"Beauty of motion" is in this splendid Packard accompanied by a beauty of design that adds to the satisfying delight of the fine sport of Twin Six motoring.

Seventeen distinctive styles in open and enclosed cars in the Third Series Twin Six—3-25 and 3-35

A s k   t h e   m a n   w h o   o w n s   o n e

Packard Motor Car Company, Detroit

Packard TWIN·6

Packard Motor Car Company. 1918.

THE FRANKLIN SEDAN

The first sedan to be introduced to the public as a regular model was the Franklin. This was in 1914. Today the sedan is the most desired type of car, and demand for the Franklin increases faster than for any other fine automobile.

20 miles to the gallon of gasoline
12,500 miles to the set of tires
50% slower yearly depreciation

FRANKLIN AUTOMOBILE COMPANY, SYRACUSE, N. Y.

Franklin Automobile Company, 1920.

McCallum Hosiery Company
[catalog cover]. c.1922.

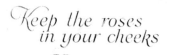

Keep the roses in your cheeks

Use

Colgate's Charmis Cold Cream for cleanliness comfort, charm. Whether out in the nipping cold of Placid, or under Palm Beach's sunny skies, your complexion can weather the weather with the help of Colgate's Cold Cream.

Colgate-Palmolive Company. 1920.

MASON CORDS

IN every community, men of broad experience and women of fine perceptions, have learned that the lasting thing is the thing of *true value*. And so, in their homes you find expressions of rare craftsmanship. And on their finest cars —Mason Cords. In short, their every possession reflects that ceaseless desire of its maker to attain the genuine and exceptional.

Branches in Principal Cities

THE MASON TIRE & RUBBER COMPANY. KENT, OHIO

Mason Tire & Rubber Company. 1923.

Remy Electric Company. 1924.

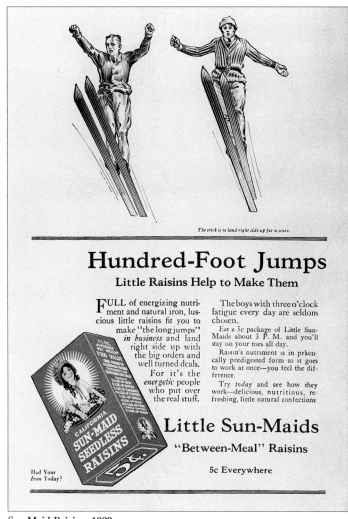

The trick is to land right side up for a score.

Hundred-Foot Jumps

Little Raisins Help to Make Them

FULL of energizing nutriment and natural iron, luscious little raisins fit you to make "the long jumps" *in business* and land right side up with the big orders and well turned deals.

For it's the *energetic* people who put over the real stuff.

The boys with three o'clock fatigue every day are seldom chosen.

Eat a 5c package of Little Sun-Maids about 3 P. M. and you'll stay on your toes all day.

Raisin's nutriment is in practically predigested form so it goes to work at once—you feel the difference.

Try *today* and see how they work—delicious, nutritious, refreshing, little natural confections.

Little Sun-Maids

"Between-Meal" Raisins

Had Your
Iron Today?

5c Everywhere

Sun-Maid Raisins. 1923.

Bristol-Myers Company. 1931.

Agile enough for a 100-foot jump

but "Pink tooth brush" can get him just the same

HOUR after hour in the biting, stinging, tonic winter air! And what joyous health is yours!

But even at that you're just as likely to get "pink tooth brush" as is the man who never *sees* the out-of-doors!

For "pink tooth brush" is the result of our preference for *soft foods*. The gums need exercise just as your muscles do. But they don't get it. They are lazy, flabby, tender gums—growing lazier and flabbier with every day—until, at length, there's "pink" upon your brush!

And gums that bleed even slightly are fair game for a host of gum troubles—gingivitis, Vincent's Disease—yes, and even for that bogy of bogies, the dreadful pyorrhea. More serious still, "pink tooth brush" is often the first step toward infection at the roots of teeth which today are so sound and healthy.

Yet there's a simple way to rid yourself of "pink tooth brush."

First, get a tube of Ipana Tooth Paste. And, each time you clean your teeth with it, put some additional Ipana on your brush and *massage it gently into your gums.* The ziratol in Ipana is the same ziratol used by the modern dentist for toning and stimulating the gums back to health.

Tomorrow—look at your teeth. Already they've lost some of their dullness. In a few days, examine your gums. Firmer, aren't they? Healthier? Of course they are! In a month they'll be hard and perfectly healthy. No more "pink tooth brush" for you!

IPANA TOOTH PASTE

BRISTOL-MYERS CO., Dept. L-31, 73 West Street, New York, N. Y.
Kindly send me a trial tube of IPANA TOOTH PASTE. Enclosed is a two-cent stamp to cover partly the cost of mailing and packing.

Name_____ Street_____

City_____ State_____

Philipsborn's. c.1920.

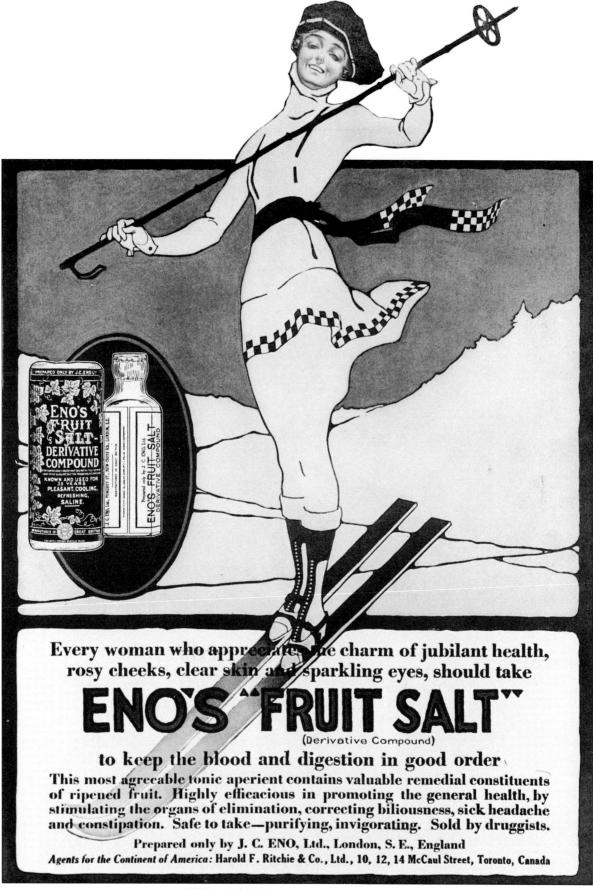

J.C. Eno, Ltd. 1918.

FOR HEALTH AND HAPPINESS ALL SEASONS THROUGH

Before Coca-Cola nobody thought it possible to produce a drink people would enjoy equally winter and summer. It took a pure drink of natural flavors ~ with that feel-good taste and delightful after-sense of refreshment ~ to prove it.

Over 7 million a day

I T   H A D   T O   B E   G O O D   T O   G E T   W H E R E   I T   I S

The Coca-Cola Company. 1927.

American Tobacco Company. 1934.

J.J. Milburn Co.
OPPOSITE HIPPODROME THEATRE
NAPA, CALIFORNIA

© R.S.B.   **January, 1925**   PAINTED BY ERNEST KULBERG

J.J. Milburn Co. 1925.

You'll do it better on *Dated* coffee

Science says coffee sweeps the cobwebs from your brain, removes fatigue and actually makes your muscles respond more quickly. But, look out for *stale* coffee!

FOR four centuries men of letters and men of action have used coffee as a stimulant. As they sipped the tempting, aromatic beverage, it gave them sure, quick exhilaration.

But there were unpleasant whispers, too. To some people coffee brought depression. If you drank too much, it made you nervous. Some people even said it gave them indigestion.

Now science has stepped in and cleared it all up.

Science has found that the people who were having trouble were probably drinking *stale* coffee!

Stale coffee develops a rancid oil. About half a cup of it to a pound. And the regular drinking of stale coffee often *does* cause indigestion, nerves, sleeplessness.

But *fresh* coffee can be drunk and enjoyed by normal, healthy grown-ups without the slightest bad effect—up to 5 cups a day!

That is why Chase & Sanborn instituted *Dated* Coffee. Insured for everyone the wonderful, healthful exhilaration that only *fresh* coffee can give.

You know Chase & Sanborn's is fresh because the date of delivery to your grocer is clearly printed on every pound. Look for it. No can of Chase & San-

born's Dated Coffee is allowed to stay on your grocer's shelf more than 10 days!

Keep away from *stale* coffee! Ask for Chase & Sanborn's Dated Coffee tomorrow. And feel how—at once—Dated Coffee picks you up. Science says, whether you're cleaning house or climbing snow-clad mountains, you'll do it better on *Dated Coffee!*

Standard Brands Inc. 1933.

and now for a
Milky Way

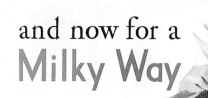

THERE'S a robust, hearty sort of satisfaction in eating a Milky Way . . . a taste thrill enjoyed by everyone, and most especially by energetic, active people. They know candy hunger at its very keenest and are best able to judge what really *satisfies* it. Watch them step up and order Milky Way.

And there are good reasons for the wonderful taste and the satisfaction found in Milky Way. That flavory center owes its goodness largely to its whole milk content and its malted milk. Then that layer of creamy caramel! Only real butter fat can give that taste. And the rich, thick milk chocolate coating, the finest grade possible to buy, is also prepared with real cows' milk.

No wonder this quality and wholesomeness are reflected in its taste. Imagine how good one would taste right now!

Every shipment of ingredients for Milky Way must pass the severest of tests by the Mars food chemists. It's the blending of these ingredients, the skill and carefulness of manufacture, that give that delightful, *satisfying* taste. Taken from any viewpoint you choose, there never has been a candy value like Milky Way.
MARS, INC., 2019-2059 N. Oak Park Ave., Chicago

NOTHING EVEN COMES CLOSE TO IT FOR SATISFYING CANDY HUNGER

Mars Incorporated. 1931.

AT THE MOUNT ROYAL *in Montreal*
166 Women Guests
tell why they find this "a perfect soap for the skin"

WINTER SPORTS at Mount Royal—

A crystal world—diamond-bright air—fields of snow that sparkle with a million tiny flames —

Men and women in love with life, as they skate, ski, toboggan, against the cold, warm in their glistening furs . . .

They go from tropical seas to twenty degrees of frost, these pleasure-loving women of the leisure class—yet manage to achieve a skin always smooth, soft, flawless in texture.

How do they do it? What soap do they find, pure enough and fine enough to keep their skin in perfect condition summer and winter?

We asked 270 women guests at beautiful Mount Royal in Montreal what soap they use for the care of their skin.

166 answered, *"Woodbury's Facial Soap!"*

"Soothing—delightful—refreshing," they said. "The only soap that does not irritate my skin." "It is all that a soap should be."—"A perfect soap!"

A SKIN SPECIALIST worked out the formula by which Woodbury's Facial Soap is made. This formula not only calls for the purest and finest ingredients; it also demands greater refinement in the manufacturing process than is commercially possible with ordinary toilet soap.

A 25-cent cake of Woodbury's lasts a month or six weeks. Around each cake is wrapped a booklet of famous skin treatments for overcoming common skin defects.

Within a week or ten days after beginning to use Woodbury's, you will notice an improvement in your complexion. Get a cake today— begin tonight the treatment your skin needs!

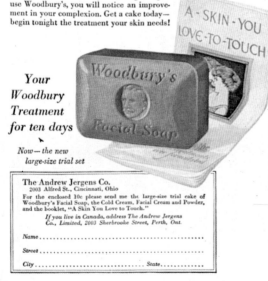

Your Woodbury Treatment for ten days

Now—the new large-size trial set

The Andrew Jergens Co.
2003 Alfred St., Cincinnati, Ohio

For the enclosed 10c please send me the large-size trial cake of Woodbury's Facial Soap, the Cold Cream, Facial Cream and Powder, and the booklet, "A Skin You Love to Touch."

If you live in Canada, address The Andrew Jergens Co., Limited, 2003 Sherbrooke Street, Perth, Ont.

Name ....

Street ....

City .... State ....

"Wrapped in furs, against the glittering background of winter—men and women in love with life . . ."

Copyright, 1926, by The Andrew Jergens Co.

Andrew Jergens Company. 1926.

Eastman Kodak Company. 1935.

Kimberly-Clark Corporation. 1930.

A GOOD RESOLUTION

—"to use nothing but Firestone Tires through-out the coming year!" Let the family enjoy the safety advantages of Gum-Dipped Balloons and the freedom from trouble that their use insures. To the woman at the wheel Firestone Tires are essential to full enjoy-ment of driving. She revels in the com-fort of the ride, confident that the wide, non-skid tread will hold in any road or boulevard — assured of freedom from slip, skid, or slide. She has the sure control of wheel and brake, so invaluable in heavy going. Let the nearest Firestone Dealer give you the benefit of his experience in tires. He will tell you why Gum-Dipped Balloons de-liver added safety and luxurious riding with the long mileage which will produce a big saving in your budget. See him today.

MOST MILES PER DOLLAR

AMERICANS SHOULD PRODUCE THEIR OWN RUBBER . *Harvey S. Firestone*

Firestone Tire and Rubber Company. 1928.

Texaco Incorporated. 1927.

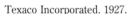

Ready to go—
with an engine that defies the cold

Golden Texaco flows . . . flows at zero . . . flows *freely* when many motor oils lag dangerously.

Brief starting seconds—the short time you spend "warming up" a cold engine—may cause more harm than hours of high-speed driving. For motor oil must flow and feed *instantly*, else pistons ride cylinder walls rough-shod, and metal grips metal harshly—destructively.

Only an oil as alert as Texaco—free of paraffin wax, of tars and cylinder stock, free of all cold-sluggish sub-stances—can give instant protection. *No matter how cold the engine may be, Texaco Motor Oil never hesitates.*

Stop at any Texaco Service Station—the Red Star and Green T identifies it. Insist upon the *correct* grade of Texaco Motor Oil.

THE TEXAS COMPANY, 17 Battery Place, New York City
Texaco Petroleum Products

TEXACO
CLEAN CLEAR GOLDEN
MOTOR OIL

A FINER AND FAR MORE DISTINGUISHED LaSALLE
. . . at an even more moderate price

It was an occasion for great rejoicing among men and women who admire fine possessions when the new La Salle V-Eight appeared upon the American scene a few weeks ago. For here was something they had been seeking. Here was a motor car of proud lineage, enriched throughout in its quality—yet offered at prices in perfect keeping with the current economic scheme. . . . No need to question the correctness of the youthful grace which is the dominating note in its appearance—for the style of the new La Salle was created by the most accomplished designers at the command of the Fisher studios. No need to wonder about its mechanical fitness or the nature of its performance—for La Salle is the product of the same skilled craftsmen who build those magnificent motor cars, the Cadillac V-Eight, V-Twelve, and V-Sixteen. . . . The new La Salle is powered by the 115-horsepower Cadillac V-type eight-cylinder engine. Throughout chassis and body are many refinements and developments of major importance, including the new Fisher No-Draft Ventilation system, individually controlled. Yet the standard five-passenger sedan is now reduced to $2245, f.o.b. Detroit—a price most attractively reasonable for a car of Cadillac design, Cadillac construction, and genuine Cadillac quality.

La Salle V-8
A GENERAL MOTORS VALUE

General Motors Incorporated. 1933.

General Motors Incorporated. 1928.

Le Sport à St. Moritz

REFRESHING FREEDOM FROM THE COMMONPLACE

To La Salle belongs all the alluring fascination which spells refreshing freedom from the commonplace. It is set apart by the same degree of charm and brilliant originality which distinguishes world famous resorts. In no car are ease and elegance more highly developed—but owners measure the La Salle in terms far beyond ease and elegance. They know that no power plant ever gave such soaring and sparkling performance as the 90-degree, V-type, 8-cylinder engine. And they know that on mountain-side or straight-away; in city traffic or rough country going, La Salle leaves the miles behind with a delightful verve peculiarly its own.

La Salle motor cars, in seventeen body styles, are priced from $2495 to $2895, f. o. b. Detroit. You may possess a La Salle on the liberal term-payment plan of the General Motors Acceptance Corporation—the appraisal value of your car acceptable as cash

LA SALLE
PRODUCT OF GENERAL MOTORS

CADILLAC MOTOR CAR COMPANY—DETROIT, MICHIGAN, AND OSHAWA, CANADA

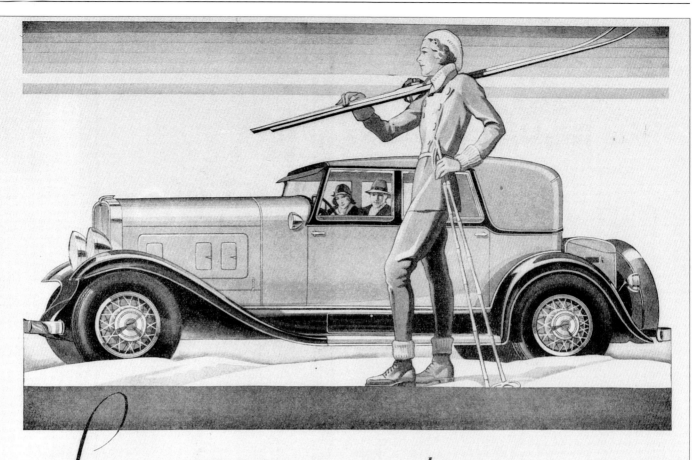

Luxurious smoothness

ACHIEVED THROUGH NEW AIR-COOLED POWER

Air-cooled power is LUXURY POWER. In the new Franklin airplane-type engine there is the luxury of extraordinary ability — the Franklin engine produces more power for size than any other automotive power plant . . . There is the luxury of greater smoothness and quietness. Ranging from a lazy idle, scarcely audible, to more than 80, you feel the remarkable absence of the vibrations and sensations usually accompanying rapid acceleration and high speed — riding is like gliding and 80 hardly seems like 50 . . . There is the luxury of worryless motor travel — no water to boil, freeze or leak.

Dietrich-styled, the De Luxe Franklin suggests custom design. Long, low appearing, airplane streamlining, air-foil fenders, and airplane windshield — airplane clear-vision and airplane instrument panel — dashing accents in gleaming, chromium-plated hood grille and port-type louvers . . . Also spacious interiors with wider seats and doors, and exquisite library upholstery. Here is a car whose heritage of elegance and dignity is immediately apparent . . . a car as modern and distinguished as the newest fast pursuit plane . . . a car eminently of the world of good taste. Franklin Automobile Company, Syracuse, New York.

SERIES FIFTEEN
in two smart lines — Trans-
continent, $2295 upward —
De Luxe, $2695 upward.
All prices f.o.b. the factory.

FRANKLIN

Franklin Automobile Company. 1931.

IMPORTANT IMPROVEMENTS

but not one change in fundamentals

The improvements and refinements incorporated in Oldsmobile illustrate effectively Olds Motor Works' policy of " . . . change only for the sake of progress—never for the sake of change alone."

The characteristic lines of the car have not been changed. The splendid engine which is responsible for the spirit and dash of Oldsmobile performance is substantially the same. The fine chassis which has so completely proved its stamina and reliability is not radically different.

Yet important advancements have been made in the body, in the engine, and in the chassis . . . improvements which definitely add to Oldsmobile comfort, luxury, efficiency, and value.

The body contours have been refined, resulting in longer, lower, smarter appearance. Interiors are more spacious and more luxurious, with finer upholsteries and more comfortable seats. Improved carburetion adds to engine efficiency. Easier steering and improved, fully-enclosed four-wheel brakes increase the stamina and dependability of the sturdy Oldsmobile chassis.

These improvements are important. They make Oldsmobile a better car and a greater value. But they do not affect, in any way, those broad fundamentals of design and construction which have made Oldsmobile so popular everywhere.

Make it a point to visit your Oldsmobile-Viking dealer and inspect this car. Ask the opinion of Oldsmobile owners. Then, when you know all the facts, you will see that Oldsmobile is, beyond question, a wise, conservative and desirable investment in motoring satisfaction.

TO DESIGN PROGRESSIVELY — TO BUILD FAITHFULLY — TO SELL HONESTLY — TO SERVICE SINCERELY

OLDSMOBILE

PRODUCT OF GENERAL MOTORS

General Motors Incorporated. 1930.

There is a **NEW TYPE** *in Motordom*

HUDSON'S Great 8

It supersedes all Hudson achievements of the past
It sells in Hudson's well-known price range

This is a new type. This is Hudson's Great 8. So tremendous its advancements that Hudson's famous achievements of the past are unhesitatingly set aside to produce it.

The motoring world thoroughly understands that no ordinary car or merely conventional eight would be entrusted to take up the onward stride of Hudson leadership. How searching, then, the tests, and supreme the proofs that we have required of it.

It is a complete new car throughout. New ideas, new beauties, new comforts, with Hudson's same price advantage. Important in principle is the relation of horse-power to car weight. It accounts for unusual alertness in get-away and in speed. It contributes much to operation economy.

Here, then, is performance more flexible and smooth in all ranges than any in Hudson's famous past. Here is quicker get-away and greater hill climbing ability. Here is a motor so smooth and powerful that it imparts a new riding sensation—active, free, effortless. You are first away at the signal to "Go!" You can relax and enjoy your ride at whatever speed you elect.

Every chassis detail is newly designed. It conforms to no standardization. It is wholly Hudson and wholly individual. Gears shift faster and freer. Roadability is increased by lower center weight, sturdy new type frame and two-way shock absorbers.

Equal distinction marks appearance. Bodies in modernistic design have new contours, new finishes. Radiator, fenders, body moldings, interior trim and fittings all blend in the new mode. Even design and treatment of windshield opener, instrument board with engine starter, fuel gauges, speedometer, adjustable seats, disappearing rear window curtain, mirror, lights, door handles, etc., are carried out in the same feeling. You will be impressed with the thoroughness and finesse of these details.

Individuality and distinction is outstanding. There is such a wide variety of colors that buyers can make their own personal selection.

Only a car possessing these qualities in preeminent degree could earn the right to carry on Hudson leadership. It sells in Hudson's well-known price range. It must continue Hudson's reputation for producing the world's greatest value. And it questions the wisdom of ever paying more for any car.

NEW MOTOR · · NEW CHASSIS · · NEW BODIES · · NEW THROUGHOUT

Hudson. 1930.

Higher Compression with *an*

Plus Willys-Knight Silence, Velvet Smoothness, Graceful Lines, Rich Colors

Willys-Knight offers you all the advantages of high compression—greater speed, flashier activity—with none of the disadvantages. Only the patented Knight sleeve-valve engine, because of the fundamental principle of its design—spherical head and sliding sleeves, which have always pro-

vided the most efficient compression chamber—gives highest *uniform* compression at all times, at all speeds—and with *any* gas!

For high, sustained efficiency, mile after mile, year after year, the Knight-powered car has set high standards all its own. The patented, exclusive Knight sleeve-valve engine is the *only* type of automobile power plant that actually grows smoother and quieter with use.

Unlike most o improvements, common to prac Knight sleeve-va property of a sing

See and drive th earliest opportun added to that of Once a Knight o

Willys-Knight Great Six 5-passenger Sedan at Lake Placid, in the Adirondacks

Gas !

portant motor car
ve rapidly become
cars, the patented
e has remained the
zation.

illys-Knight, at your
enthusiasm will be
han 300,000 owners.
ays a Knight owner.

BEAUTIFUL NEW COLORS

Your choice of many exquisitely distinctive new color combinations, both in lacquer and upholstery. Colors
that are rich, harmoniously blended, lastingly attractive—outstanding ensembles of rare taste and artistry.

WILLYS-KNIGHT

$1295
f.o.b. factory

is all you pay for a 5-passenger, 6-cylinder Willys-Knight closed car. "70"
Six, $1295 to $1495. Great Six, $1850 to $2695. Prices f.o.b. factory and
specifications subject to change without notice. Willys-Overland, Inc.,
Toledo, Ohio. Willys-Overland Sales Co., Ltd., Toronto, Canada.

Willys-Overland Inc. 1927.

England. 1918.

HISTORY OF THE PICTURE POSTCARD

"When archaeologists of the thirtieth century begin to excavate...ruins..., they will focus their attention on the picture postcard as the best means of penetrating the spirit of the...era. They will collect and collate thousands of these cards and they will reconstruct our epoque from the strange hieroglyphics and images they reveal, spared by the passage of time."

James Douglas
English journalist, 1907

Picture postcards originated in Europe in the early 1870s. Production increased in the 1890s with the introduction of new printing techniques and the extension of licenses to private industry to publish postcards. Collotype printing became available on an industrial scale, which led to a proliferation of photographic postcards and color lithography.

Social and cultural factors encouraged the growth of the postcard well into the twentieth century. The brevity of the verbal message and the presence of the illustration to augment the written word, by amplifying its meaning or charging it with allusions, were among the reasons for the extraordinary popularity of postcards.

The appearance of the postcard brought about some interesting changes in Victorian and Edwardian letter-writing habits. A letter's contents were concealed inside an envelope, which was considered an improper means of communication for young lovers. A postcard, on the other hand, made it possible to inspect what was written and was therefore more acceptable.

"Like many great inventions," observed the English journalist James Douglas in 1907, "the postcard has brought a silent revolution in our habits. It has freed us unexpectedly from the fatigue of writing letters. There is no space for courtesy."

The postcard became a means of picturesque documentation at a low price, and it was coveted by millions of collectors worldwide. Postcards served as a substitute for those who could not afford first-hand experiences of the places and subjects represented in them. At the turn of the century, postcard stalls or kiosks were a common sight in public gardens and exhibition parks in European cities, as were postcard salesmen passing along trains, or from table to table in cafes and restaurants.

Before 1907 writing was not permitted on the address and stamp side of the postcard (the reverse side of the graphic). Senders of cards had to write their message over the image on the front (graphic) side. In 1907 it became permissible for the writer to use the newly created divided back side for the message, keeping the graphic

Typical greeting card. c.1915.

image clean for the recipient and for posterity.

The golden age of the picture postcard ran from 1898 to the end of the First World War in 1918. During those twenty years many artists and photographers in Europe, the United States and elsewhere developed graphics for postcard publishers. The postcard brought both art and the photographic experience within the range of the masses.

Women assumed a central role in postcard iconography, and they were popularized by postcard artists in many different situations. Artists often escaped into fantasy with their symbolic and sublime elevation of womankind into idealized beings of perfection. Significantly, the woman was the principal subject in most illustrators' work, even when there was a man at her side.

Children also figured prominently in picture postcards throughout the world. In most cases, the image of childhood, with its uninhibited joy in living, its implicit message of hope for the future, and its innocence and openness, was bound up with the message or greeting on the postcard: Happy Christmas, Happy Easter, Happy New Year, and so on.

Sport in general, including skiing, has always been a major theme of picture postcards. Participatory sport emerged as a new phenomenon around the turn of the century, its mass appeal becoming synonymous with modernism. Sport was a heroic activity, and skiing became an intensely popular postcard subject worldwide.

The postcard was also a means of promoting or reflecting trends in current fashion. As such, postcards are valuable records of ski fashions for both men and women throughout the historic period covered in this volume.

With the availability of photographic postcards, ski scenery became a popular subject for many postcard publishers, bringing the viewer closer to the exciting life at ski resorts. Many sports resorts, recognizing the benefits of worldwide attention and publicity, published their own skiing picture postcards to promote their tourist facilities and to further the glamorous appeal of the sport.

Postcards became important documents for revealing the international spread of skiing as a popular sport. Without the availability of this media, much of the populace would have had no resource for discovering the excitement of skiing.

While collections of postcards in public museums do exist today, the collection of cards is primarily the domain of individuals who buy and trade for cards, much as their grandparents did generations ago. Now many collectors also do so to preserve and record the history of times past.

When viewed closely, each postcard in this collection has a story to tell. The scenery, characters and action scenes are static, but they can be brought to life vividly with a bit of imagination and with close attention to the depictions of clothing styles, ski equipment and locations. Through close observation these images can greatly enhance our concept of skiing as it existed from the turn of the century to 1936.

Woman skier. 1921.

Belgium. 1912.

Italy. c.1915.

Austria. 1905.

La Porte, California, USA. 1905.

USA. c.1905.

LAPPER PAA SKI

Norway. c.1902.

USA. c.1905.

La Porte, California, USA. 1911.

9705 - Ski-Sport

Switzerland. 1909.

Switzerland. c.1908.

Switzerland. 1906.

Australia. 1913.

Australia. c.1910.

Norway. 1907.

France. c.1910.

Belgium. 1910.

Belgium. c.1908.

Europe. c.1910.

Slik ser de norske sportsdamer ut.

Norway. 1912.

Austria. 1912.

France. 1913.

Austria. 1913.

Belgium. 1909.

Austria. 1912.

Switzerland. c.1905.

Germany. 1914.

USA. c.1920.

France. c.1910.

France. c.1910.

France. c.1910.

Norway. c.1905.

Norway. 1907.

Germany. 1912.

Switzerland. c.1930.

Norway. 1916.

Switzerland. c.1910.

Wintersport in Celerina.

Die Kronprinzessin und Prinzessin Viktoria Luise.

Germany. 1913.

18351 St. Moritz — Skikjöring

Switzerland. 1912.

Switzerland. c.1915.

Switzerland. c.1915.

J. J. 8032 Armée Suisse, Skieurs

Switzerland. 1912.

LES CHASSEURS ALPINS DANS LES VOSGES... Chaussés de skis, ils font sur les pentes neigeuses des charges foudroyantes à la baïonnette

France. c.1910.

Lake Placid, New York, USA. 1921.

Lake Placid, New York, USA. c.1930.

Lake Placid, New York, USA. 1921.

Switzerland. c.1915.

Switzerland. c.1915.

Canada. c.1920.

Switzerland. 1919.

Belgium. 1908.

Belgium. 1908.

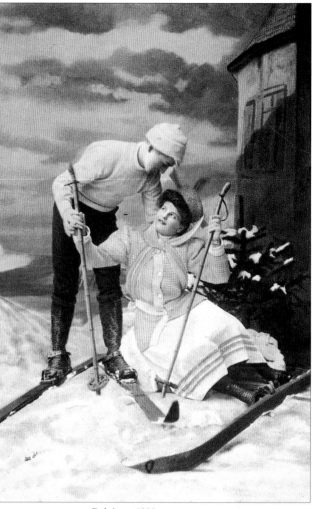

Belgium. 1908.

Belgium. 1908.

Norway. 1913.

Norway. 1908.

Europe. 1915.

Europe. 1917.

Italy. c.1910

Italy. c.1910

Italy. c.1910

Italy. c.1910

Austria. c.1915.

Austria. c.1915.

England. c.1910.

Switzerland. 1911.

Virginia, Minnesota, USA. c.1915.

Ski Tournament, Duluth, Minn.

Duluth, Minnesota, USA. c.1908.

Ishpeming, Mich.   National Skee Tournament.

Ishpeming, Michigan, USA. c.1908.

Norway. 1916.

Norway. 1907.

Norway. c.1910.

Norway. 1909.

Norway. c.1910.

Norway. 1908.

Norway. 1908.

Norway. c.1903.

Austria. 1902.

Europe. c.1910.

Switzerland. c.1915.

Switzerland. c.1915.

Switzerland. c.1915.

Switzerland. c.1915.

England. 1911.

Sweden. c.1910.

Norway. c.1903.

Norway. c.1910.

Europe. c.1920.

England. c.1910.

France. c.1910.

St. Paul, Minnesota, USA. 1917.

Wenn das man gut geht!

Europe. c.1915.

Nachtfahrt

Europe. c.1915.

England. c.1910.

Germany. 1909.

Switzerland. c.1910.

Switzerland. 1911.

Switzerland. c.1910.

Norway. c.1901.

Norway. 1903.

Glædelig Jul godt
Nytaar.
Magna Nærup

Norway. 1903.

"*En glædelig jul* "!
Yours sincerely
Anna Margarete Bödtke

Norway. c.1903.

Norway. 1904.

Norway. c.1910.

USA. c.1910.

Canada. c.1910.

England. 1916.

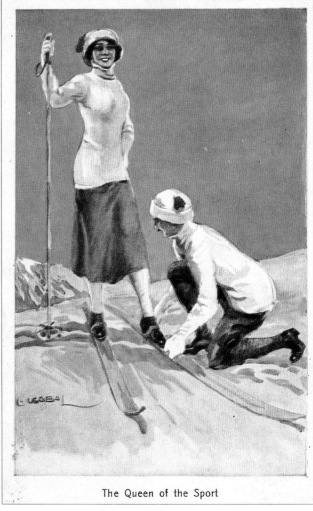

The Queen of the Sport

Germany. 1910.

Norway. 1911.

Canada. 1913.

Germany. c.1910.

Germany. c.1910.

Switzerland. 1909.

Canada. 1911.

France. c.1910.

Germany. 1910.

USA. c.1910.

USA. 1910.

USA. 1911.

USA. 1912.

Sweden. 1902.

England. c.1910.

Germany. c.1915.

Corneille Max   Winter

Germany. c.1915.

Austria. 1913.

Germany. c.1910.

Germany. c.1915.

SCHNEESCHUH-PATROUILLE   OTTO FLECHTNER

PROSIT NEUJAHR 1916!

Germany. 1915.

Norway. c.1903.

Switzerland. 1909.

USSR. c.1920.

Norway. c.1905.

スキー隊の連鎖　(冬の小樽)

Japan. c.1930.

Unitas -Bindung — Feinverpassung
Unitas -Strammer — Beste Fassung
Unitas ist Dir — Freudbereitung
Unitas bringt Dir — Ski-Hochleistung!

Europe. c.1925.

Sweden. c.1920.

Europe. c.1915.

Germany. 1936.

Germany. 1936.

A tous les âges de la vie, l'HÉMOSTYL du Docteur ROUSSEL donne des forces.
Op alle levensperioden schenkt HEMOSTYL van Dokter ROUSSEL kracht.

Belgium. c.1920.

France. c.1925.

France. c.1925.

France. c.1925.

UNIQUE CHAIR SKI LIFTS AT SUN VALLEY, IDAHO

Sun Valley, Idaho, USA. 1936.

SKIING IN SUN VALLEY'S POWDERED SNOW   FROM KODACHROME

Sun Valley, Idaho, USA. 1936.

Sun Valley, Idaho, USA. 1936.

Sun Valley, Idaho, USA. 1936.

Italy. c.1925.

Italy. c.1925.

Italy. c.1925.

Italy. c.1925.

ACKNOWLEDGEMENTS

All original materials included in this book are from the personal collection of the author, Gary Schwartz. The materials are reproduced and acknowledged as stated below. While the publisher makes every effort possible to publish full and correct credits for each work included in this volume, sometimes errors may occur. The publisher regrets any such errors but must disclaim any liablility.

ADVERTISERS:

Ansco Photo-Optical Products Corporation.
Coca-Cola. Permission for use of ads granted by The Coca-Cola Company.
Colgate-Palmolive Company.
Firestone. The Firestone Tire & Rubber Company.
Graflex Inc.
Kodak. Reprinted courtesy of Eastman Kodak Company. Copyright by Eastman Kodak Company.
Kotex. KOTEX is a trademark of Kimberly-Clark Corporation. Reprinted with permission.
Mars Incorporated.
Packard. To the extent Cooper Industries owns rights.
Studebaker. To the extent Cooper Industries owns rights.
Sun-Maid Growers of California.
Texaco Incorporated.

MAGAZINES:

The American Legion Magazine.
Child Life Magazine. Copyright 1934, 1962 by Rand McNally & Company.
Harper's.
Ladies' Home Journal. Copyrights 1929, 1931, 1934, 1935, Meredith Corporation. All rights reserved.
The New Yorker. Copyright 1935, 1963. The New Yorker Magazine, Inc..
Pictorial Review.
Saturday Evening Post. Reprinted from the Saturday Evening Post, Copyright 1928, 1935, The Curtis Publishing Co.
Vogue. Copyrights c1931 (renewed 1959) by The Conde Nast Publications Inc.

INDEX

Adelboden, Switzerland 11
Advertising history 23, 71-73
Aeneid (Virgil's) 9
Alta, Utah 16
Alturas Snowshoe Club 13
Arlberg ski method 12
Army skiing 9, 11
Australia 10
Austria 11, 16

Berthoud Pass, Colorado 16
Brighton, Utah 16

California 12, 13, 16
Carson Valley, California 13
Chairlift history 17
Chamonix, France 12
Children (as subjects) 103
Christiania (Oslo), Norway 10, 12
Christiania turn 11
Colorado 12, 16

Dartmouth Outing Club 14
Davos, Switzerland 11
Dyer, Rev. John L. 12

Equipment and clothing 14-15

Fashion 14-15, 103
Foster's Hill, Shawbridge, Canada 15

Germany 11
Graphic illustration 7, 21-23, 72
Greenland 10, 11
Grindelwald, Switzerland 11

Haakonson, King Haakon (Norway) 9
Hannagan, Steve 16
Harriman, W. Averell 16
Harris, Fred 14

International Federation of Skiing 12
Ishpeming, Michigan 13

"J" Bar 16
Jackson Hole, Wyoming 16

Ketchum, Idaho (Sun Valley) 16-17

Lake Placid, New York 12, 15
Lake Placid Club 15
Lake Tahoe 16
La Porte, California 13
Lillienfeld ski school 11

Mt. Rainier, Washington 16
Mt. Hood, Oregon 16
Magazine history 21-23
    Frank Leslie's Illustrated Weekly 22
    Harper's Weekly 22
    Life 23

Michigan 13
Midwest (U.S.) 13, 14
Minnesota 13

Nansen, Fridtjof 11
National Ski Association (United States Ski
    Association) 14
New England (U.S.) 13
New Hampshire 14
Nordheim, Sondre 10, 13
Norway 9, 10, 13

Olympic Games (Winter) 12, 15
Oregon 16

Peary, Robert E. 10
Placerville, California 13
Postcard history 102-103

Racing 12, 13
Rocky Mountain National Park, Colorado 16
Rope tow history 15-16

St. Moritz, Switzerland 16
San Bernardino Mountains, California 16
Scandinavia 9
Schaffgotsch, Count Felix 16
Scenery (as subject) 103
Schneider, Hannes 11-12
Schniebs, Otto 14
Sierra mining camps 13
Ski Club of Great Britain 11
Skis, or snowshoes 10, 11, 12, 13, 14
Ski poles 11
Snow trains 14, 16
Sports (as subject) 103
Stem-christie 11
Stretcher 9
Switzerland 11, 16
Sun Valley, Idaho 16-17, 23
Sweden 9

Telemark turn 10
Thompson, John A. ("Snowshoe") 12-13

United States Eastern Amateur Ski
    Association 14
Utah 12, 16

Vasa, Gustav 9
Virgil 9

Warfare on skis 9
Wisconsin 13
Women (as subjects) 103
Woodstock, Vermont (Gilbert's Hill) 15

Yosemite National Park 16

Zdarsky, Mathias 11, 14
Zion National Park, Utah 16